THE WORLD

is Our Lab

Jessica Sanders

Kendall Hunt
publishing company

www.kendallhunt.com
Send all inquiries to:
4050 Westmark Drive
Dubuque, IA 52004-1840

Table of Contents

Preface

How Did I Find Sociology?

Sociology is one of the greatest loves of my life. I came to find my love for Sociology by way of enrolling in an elective course while an undergraduate at West Virginia University. This course intrigued me, though I knew nothing about it or the field of study. The title of this course? Introduction to Sociology. This course happens to be the same one you may now find yourself in. . . . It turns out I now teach this course more than any other in my professional career. I taught it for the first time 11 years ago, and cannot even count the number of sections I have taught in person and online for a variety of colleges and universities since then. My love for it continues to grow, and each time I teach it I learn from my students and their unique life experiences and perspectives. I hope to bring some of the magic of this course to your life.

What I Found While Taking the Course—I was Already Thinking Like a Sociologist!

Instead of being intimidated by a subject I previously knew nothing about, I very quickly realized Sociology came naturally to me. In fact, I was already thinking about the world, and asking Sociological questions, without even realizing I was doing so. What does that mean? It means I look at the world around me, and the people in it, and seek to understand. I ask questions such as "Why does this happen?" and also "How can we change this?" I question inequality, and refuse to give up on the potential for progress to be made. We can live a better life, and the world can change, power to the people comes through the Sociological method.

Sociology Enriches All Lives, Regardless of Your Major or Career Path

It doesn't matter if you never find yourself in another Sociology course, the magic of the Intro course will enrich your life. I promise. This is one of the core reasons I find this course so fulfilling from my end. I have the chance to teach future medical doctors, lawyers, and engineers. All professions will benefit from a Sociological understand. A deepening of the desire to see where the other person is coming from will make one a more empathetic and successful professional, regardless of their industry.

Keep an Open Mind, and the Intro Course Will Change You

All it takes for Sociology to change you is the willingness to allow the process to work—to start from utilizing the Sociological perspective and shed your own biases. Culture shock does not have to be a way of life, and we don't have to stay ethnocentric. We can change our own selves, and then our own cultures, and then the entire social world, through the correct usage of Sociology. That is the mission I am on, and I am pleased to have you join me on this path.

Acknowledgments

To Mom and Dad, for your never-ending support and wisdom, without which I would never have had the strength and endurance to follow the academic path.

To my Soul Sisters, for holding space for me and allowing me the courage to reach for the stars.

To my Students, for teaching me new things every class, keeping me young and hip (that's my story and I'm sticking with it), and engaging in Sociological discussions with me on even the toughest of topics.

To my dear Kendall Hunt team, Anne and Maegen, for the constant assistance and collaboration on the journey to turning my Soul's mission into a tangible piece of literary manifestation.

CHAPTER 1
Introduction

1. What Is Sociology? A Social Science That Studies Groups of People
2. The WORLD Is Our Lab. We Can Look at All Topics Sociologically
3. Must Use Sociological Imagination—Get Past Own Biases. Do Not Be Ethnocentric. You Can Experience Culture Shock
4. Look at Sociological Issues from All Perspectives: Culture, Structure, and Power
5. Founders of Sociology: *Durkheim, Weber, Marx, W.E.B. Du Bois, Jane Addams*

Welcome to Sociology. I take it some of you are here because you plan to do more studies in the field of Sociology; however, I am going to make a guess about the rest of you. Perhaps you are taking this as a general education requirement? Rest assured that even if Sociology is not your intended career or field of study, you will be pleasantly surprised to find it applies to all areas of life. One of the most fun things about teaching Sociology for me has been finding ways to incorporate the wide variety of professional goals my students have into the course materials. You will find I took great care to have that same focus with this text as well.

I always warn my students to stick with me through the first two chapters of the course. Chapter 1 is the key background knowledge—relevant terms, basic framework, important people, and an understanding of what in the world this term "Sociology" is. Chapter 2 will provide you with the research framework. It is important to point out that Sociology is in fact a science. Our field of study belongs to a specific type of science you may not have dealt with before, Social Sciences. We use the same Scientific Method as the natural sciences, in that we always start from a topic of interest. We then come up with a hypothesis, composed of a dependent variable and independent variable. More on that to come.

1. What Is Sociology? A Social Science That Studies Groups of People

So where do we begin our studies? How about where I often like to go—a real-world example. Have you ever looked at something going on in the world and asked, "WHY?" This is Sociology in action. An example I have often found myself asking is "Why do some people leave the shopping carts in a parking space when they are done shopping?" Ever have this happen to you? For some reason, this seems to affect me every time. I see a close-up parking space, go to turn into it, and bam—what is in the way? A shopping cart! Now let's combine this issue with Sociology.

5AM Images/Shutterstock.com

Sociology is the scientific study of groups of people. You can ask various questions once you identify a Sociological issue. So, for example, with the shopping cart example, you can ask "*Who is leaving the shopping carts in parking spaces?*" There you might ask—is it a gender issue? Is it an age issue? Is it a social class issue? You could also ask a why question—"*Why are people leaving shopping carts in parking spaces*?" Perhaps they are in a hurry? Maybe they are oblivious to the fact this behavior has a negative impact on those around them? Or perhaps they don't care at all who their behavior impacts? You could also ask "*When are people most likely to leave shopping carts in parking spaces?*" Is this behavior impacted by the weather—perhaps rainy or snowy day has the highest rates of this? Each of these questions is a valid Sociological question on a valid Sociological topic. The type of question you ask will determine the type of data collection method you will use, the type of data you will collect, and the way you will analyze the data.

It is important to note **Sociology** studies groups of people and the social world. It is a Social Science and we use the Scientific Method in our field. You will learn more about how to do that in Chapter 2. You can look at almost any topic from a Sociological lens, and *the world is our lab*.

2. The WORLD Is Our Lab. We *Can* Look at All Topics Sociologically

Think of any topic in the social world. Guess what? You can analyze it Sociologically. Don't believe me? Let's go through some examples. First off, you want to consider which topics work best in a Sociological analysis. Compare Sociology to a closely related Social Science,

Psychology. In Psychology, research and analysis is often focused on the individual. In Sociology, we are more concerned with mass behavior. Social movements work great for analysis, as do large trends.

If you wanted to conduct some analysis on a drug-related issue, you would have a wide variety of illegal drugs to choose from. Marijuana would be one in particular where you would find a great deal of data to analyze. We know that even though this drug is illegal in most

Canna Obscura/Shutterstock.com

places in the United States, we still have a society and culture that can encourage the use of this drug in many ways—think of music, fashion, movies, and so on.

On the other hand, if you saw a news report on the use of bath salts and the zombie-like behavior it causes, that is, reports of people eating the faces of their victims, you might think—"Wow! What an extreme reaction, this will surely be a great Sociological topic!" But not so fast. Though this topic may sound interesting, this is a drug which is not as widely used as marijuana. The dramatic side effects will be interesting for a news report, but you will struggle to obtain enough data to make any serious Sociological study.

Instead of looking at small, uncommon occurrences in society it would be better for you to spend your time studying a social movement.

So, perhaps your next question is, what are **Social movements**?

Social movements occur when groups of people get together for a common purpose. Often social movements are united around a political purpose, such as electing a certain

person to a political position. They can also be centered around a specific issue and seeking a social change. You can think about the example of the recent women's rights social media movements such as the MeToo and other recent women's rights protests. When you look at groups of people behaving in common ways, this will give you a great Sociological topic. Remember the world is our lab, so most topics in the social world are fair game for our field.

Andrew Repp/Shutterstock.com

3.   Must Use Sociological Imagination—Get Past Own Biases. Do Not Be Ethnocentric. You Can Experience Culture Shock

When you look at issues Sociologically, this means you look at them from a more neutral viewpoint than you might normally. You want to always utilize the **Sociological imagination**. You will attempt to get beyond your own biases as much as possible, to consider the possible reasons a social phenomenon is occurring. We know that all of us have been impacted by our own life experiences, affected by our own cultures, and thus we have formed our own ideas about the world. These ideas can include what is right or wrong, what is desirable or undesirable, and more. It is important when using the Sociological imagination to place these ideas to the side, and step into the role of a Sociologist. Attempt to analyze the issue from all angles.

4.   Look at Sociological Issues from All Perspectives: Culture, Structure, and Power Analysis

There are three main lenses you will always want to consider when analyzing an issue Sociologically, and they are: culture, structure, and power. The easiest way to understand all three, and the relationship between them, is by taking us through an example, so let's do just that.

DisobeyArt/Shutterstock.com

For our example, we will look at the current complaint many older people in society have about the younger generations—"overuse of technology, specifically cell phones." Now, note when we say overuse here we as the Sociologists are not implying good or bad, rather pointing out the older generation is making the assumption that the amount of usage is beyond what is "normal" or "acceptable." So right away we know there are some judgments being made, and perhaps some prejudice being applied. This will often be the case with Sociological questions and topics.

Culture is everything man made in society, so everything that is not natural. Culture is impacted by geographical place and historical time period. You can look at one society and see all the changes to the culture there throughout time, or you could compare one society to others in different locations and note the differences between them.

In the cell phone use example, you would have to look at the culture in a few different ways. First, you would examine the mainstream American culture today. Are people using a lot of technology in their daily lives? Do most people have cell phones? Or is it just the younger generations? Here, you would need to begin to get more specific. You'd have to define what you mean by "a lot of use" and you would have to set a criterion for the younger generation. Are you going with teenagers, or will you be looking at an entire generation, for example, millennials?

You can also compare the culture now to the past. So, for example, you'd ask, has the culture always been this way, have people always used cell phones so much? Right away you should notice something important, there is a true time period relevance here, as cell phones have only been around for a period of time.

When you examine the geographical cultural issues for this topic, you would need to compare one area to another's culture. Again, you must get more specific here. Are you going to look at all the United States, or will you pick a specific region, state, or even town? You could compare the cell phone usage of the United States to a part of the world where they don't have a lot of access to cell phone service, though you could see how that would heavily bias your data.

Next you want to move on to examine the structure. **Structure** is the cohesive force in society. One main structure is our laws; they hold together the legal world. Then we have our norms, the social rules of behavior that hold together our social world. Without structure in society, you would have a pretty disorganized world. However, the structure in society does not always work in the way it is intended to, so oftentimes when you are analyzing the structure of a Sociological issue, you will find dysfunction.

The structure of our cell phone example could be the expected behavior. If you are saying someone is overusing the cell phone you must ask, "How much cell phone use is expected?" Is there a structure for where and when you can versus can't use a cell phone? For example, if you are home it is acceptable versus in the middle of a crowded movie theater during a movie, or versus, during a college class! Analyzing these structural issues will shed light on your topic, and help you to become informed on the related issues and possible causes.

Finally, you will want to examine the power. **Power** is all about who is in charge. Who makes the rules concerning this Sociological issue, and more importantly, who has the authority to change them? In this example, there are many power issues you could look at. Is it considered power to obtain a cell phone? We know not everyone in the world can do so, so that right there is a type of technological power we are assuming in our analysis. Another power issue would be who is determining "overuse" of cell phones? It seems in the example we stated the power is lying in the older generation's hands; they are the ones questioning the younger people's cell phone and technology usage.

Hopefully this analysis did not overwhelm you. We will delve much further into the culture, structure, power procedure, as we will apply it to many different topics throughout the book. For now, you have the basic understanding of how to look at topics like a Sociologist, and the main lenses to consider.

TypoArt BS/Shutterstock.com

5. Founders of Sociology: *Durkheim, Weber, Marx, W.E.B. Du Bois, Jane Addams*

The last topic we will cover in this chapter is the founders of Sociology.

A quick note on the use of the word "Founders" here, rather than "inventors." In Sociology, we wouldn't say anyone invented it. This is because humans have probably always been conducting Sociology, regardless of whether it was an academic category or not. There were important figures in the early stages of Sociology, and you would be expected to have a general knowledge of these key people when discussing the history of our field. I have laid out the main point for each individual.

Durkheim—Emile Durkheim, a French sociologist, is known for his concept of *anomie*, which talks about the depression people can feel when there is too little structure in society. This theory is from the late 1800s, and yet still seems to hold up in our current-day analysis of societies.

Weber—Max Weber, a German sociologist, is known for his concept of *Verstehen*. He stated it is important to look at the meaning people attach to things in order to understand their actions. You can better predict the behavior of people in society if you know what they value or believe in.

Everett Historical/Shutterstock.com

Marx—Karl Marx is perhaps the most widely recognizable founding theorist. He is responsible for Marxism, which is an alternative to Capitalism. He strongly believed Capitalism contributes to an unjust social world, and he called for a reform of society.

W.E.B. Du Bois—Du Bois was the first African American to receive a PhD from Harvard University, and he contributed a great deal to the study of racial inequality in American society. He also founded the NAACP, the National Association for the Advancement of Colored People.

Jane Addams—Jane Addams is notable as one of the first women Sociologists. She was part of the Chicago School, and founded the Hull House. Her work focused on aiding the poor, and she provided the community with educational services and arts.

Summary

Now you have the basic framework of how to think like a Sociologist! You should set your biases aside as much as possible, and utilize the Sociological imagination. Then, after you have selected a topic, be sure to examine the related issues according to: culture, structure, and power. Yes, Sociology is a science, it's a Social Science. The world is our lab. Chapter 2 will provide you with all the scientific knowledge you need to conduct your own Sociological work.

Activity 1: Pick a Topic You Would Like to Study Sociologically

*What is something you have observed in the world, and found yourself asking "Why does this happen?" or "Why does this?" or "When or where does this behavior occur?"

*Make sure you can have enough data—do many people do this? Is there a historical significance? If it is a trend, does it occur in a certain subsection of the population?

NakoPhotography/Shutterstock.com

Write your three topic choices here:

A.

B.

C.

Activity 2: Culture, Structure, Power Analysis of a Topic

Take your best topic from Activity 1.

Now analyze it Sociologically—that means to look at it through the three main lenses—**Culture, Structure, and Power**

loreanto/Shutterstock.com

1. For **Culture**, you will consider factors such as: Is this topic different in one culture versus another? Is this topic culturally acceptable, or frowned upon and judged?

2. For **Structure**, you will consider factors such as: Are there laws relevant to this topic? Are there social rules and expectations relevant to this topic?

3. For **Power**, you will consider factors such as: Who has the power in this topic? Is one group asserting their power or dominance over another? Does one group feel at a disadvantage due to power struggles?

CHAPTER 2
Conducting Sociology

1. Selecting a Topic of Interest—Inductive versus Deductive Approach
2. Setting Up Your Research
   Hypothesis, Dependent Variable, Independent Variable
3. What Type of Data Collected—Quantitative versus Qualitative
4. Do Not Infer Causation from Correlation. Ice Cream Eating and Murder Example
5. Types of Theories: Functionalist, Conflict, Symbolic Interactionist
6. How Can Sociology Help the World? Real-World Jobs, How Sociology Can Take Place in All Careers

It is best to start this chapter with a quick reminder—in Chapter 1, I warned you to stick with me through the first two, more "boring" chapters. Of course, if you were to ask me, I'd say all of Sociology is the most exciting thing ever, but I get my biased love for all things Sociology is not shared by everyone . . . Chapter 1 gave us the framework for the field. This chapter will focus on how to conduct Sociology. This means we will be learning the process of Social Science. The good news is Social Sciences use the same basic tools as all other sciences, so you will find many of these concepts will be reviewed from any other science-related course. We will walk through the decisions you must make when setting up your experiment, discuss how to avoid getting caught in the "beginner mistake"

Rawpixel.com/Shutterstock.com

11

with analyzing your results, and learn the different theory types. The chapter ends with a focus on how Sociology and the research process can be used to help the world.

1.   Selecting a Topic of Interest—Inductive versus Deductive Approach

We talked about selecting a Sociological topic in Chapter 1, and we will pick back up with that discussion now. Remember the title of our book—*The World Is Our Lab*. This means most topics can be studied using our approach. There are two types of approaches you will take to come up with your hypothesis, what you will study. Will you look at things from an inductive approach or a deductive one? **Inductive reasoning** makes broad generalization from specific observations,

mimagephotography/Shutterstock.com

whereas **deductive reasoning** starts with an idea and then seeks observations. Most of the time you will be using deductive reasoning, as you will be noticing something occurring in the social world and asking "Why is this happening?" You can also ask "Who is the one doing this thing?" or "Where is this most likely to happen?"

2.   Setting Up Your Research—Hypothesis, Dependent Variable, Independent Variable

After getting clear on your topic you will need to set it up into a testable format. In the sciences we call this statement a hypothesis. In a **hypothesis**, you will need to include two important components: a **dependent variable** (DV) and an **independent variable** (IV). The easiest way to think about it is to say your DV will hopefully be depending on your IV. So,

if you are studying something involving people, you hope something, like a reaction or belief, or type of behavior will depend on whatever else is going on. It is easiest to explain using a specific example, so let's walk through one.

I want to know why people are in worse moods when it rains. I am hoping the mood of people depends on the weather, specifically the rain. So here the DV is the mood, and it is depending on the IV, the weather, the rain. For this example I did not personally

g-stockstudio/Shutterstock.com

manipulate the weather, surprisingly that isn't within the abilities of a college professor. Keep in mind you don't have to be the one producing the IV, in fact many times you will be examining things that are already occurring in society. You need to make sure your DV and IV are as clear and specific as possible. This will help you ensure your hypothesis is testable, and can provide you with results for you to analyze.

3.   What Type of Data Collected—Quantitative versus Qualitative

The next step in your process after developing a testable hypothesis is to determine what type of data you will be collecting. You have two choices here: quantitative or qualitative data. **Quantitative data** deals with numbers and **qualitative data** can be everything nonnumerical. It is helpful to think of some examples. A common example of quantitative data would be age. Think of how important one's age would be in so many Sociological studies. Weight and height would be other quantitative data examples. Qualitative data can include opinions—so you could ask "How do you feel about the current President?" The answers you would get back would be varied, and they would be qualitative data.

4.   Do Not Infer Causation from Correlation. Ice Cream Eating and Murder Example

Now that you have a testable hypothesis and have determined what type of data you will be collecting; you need to be sure to include one very important step. Memorize the following phrase: **DO NOT INFER CAUSATION FROM CORRELATION**. To help us understand what this phrase means, let's walk it through an example.

What if I told you I found out that eating ice cream causes murder?

Would you look at me like I am a crazy person? Wouldn't you think—"Now wait a

Kseniia Perminova/Shutterstock.com

second, everyone knows eating ice cream makes people happy humans, not murderers!" The issue here is that I got caught up in a common "beginner's mistake" in Sociology, I inferred causation from correlation. True, I did see a connection with my data between my DV and my IV. But I did not check to see if one was causing the change in the other. Rather, the two variables had a relationship where they both increased together, so they did have correlation, but they were lacking causation.

In this example, to satisfy the causation requirement, the ice cream eating would have to be what was directly causing the increase in murder rates. In fact, as a researcher, I missed another factor—the weather. On warm weather days, more people eat ice cream. On warm weather days, people commit more crimes, including murder. The weather is causing the increase in murder and you are making a mistake by inferring the ice cream was the cause. The good news takeaway here is that ice cream eating is safe!

So, how do you ensure you don't make this same mistake? Is there ever a way to totally examine all related causes? No, remember our world is the lab, so there will always be many factors influencing your data. However, you can do the best you can to look for all outside influences, and take your time before jumping to a conclusion of causation simply from seeing the presence of correlation.

5.   Types of Theories: Functionalist, Conflict, Symbolic Interactionist

There are three main theory types we use in Sociology. You will approach your topic from one of these three angles. It is possible your theory will have elements of all three. The first type of theories are **Functionalist theories**. These theories deal with an area of society, and ask "Is this functioning?" For example, you could look at the system of higher education, and ask if all areas are functioning. One recent area which has fallen under criticism is the price of obtaining a college degree in the United States. Note, Functionalist theories don't only deal with something that is functioning, in fact many times they will instead be point-

ing out a dysfunction. Your theory here could be, "The cost of higher education in the United States is making it difficult for students to pay off their high student loan debt after graduation."

The next type of theories are **Conflict theories**. Conflict theories examine a conflict going on in society. Now, yes, these theories can focus on physical conflict and violence, such as war or violent crime. However, there are conflicts at all areas of society. Think of tension among different groups of people, gender stereotypes, and political disagreements. All of these could be studied under the category of Conflict theory. An example could be "What is causing such a serious divide between the Republican and Democratic parties, and why can't they simply sit down to discuss it?"

The third type of theories are **Symbolic Interactionist theories**. These theories look at the symbols we use in our society and the meaning people attach to them. I always tell my students to think about

michaeljung/Shutterstock.com

Jacob Lund/Shutterstock.com

the drug use many of us engage in—the legal drug of caffeine. When I want to give a good lecture and I am already feeling tired, I may bring in a cup of coffee to enjoy while I am teaching.

If instead of a cup of coffee I brought in a large energy drink, would my students judge me differently? I ask this question every semester and I always get the same answer—yes, the judgement there would be different. The substance I am ingesting is the same, caffeine. The effect it is having on my body and my ability to teach is the same. The difference? The form of it, and the symbol my students attach to it. Coffee equals a positive judgement in our culture, we have coffee shops and an entire industry formed around coffee. Energy drinks are popular too, but the connotation attached to them may not fit in the symbolic meaning students have for a professor. A Symbolic Interactionist theory could be "Students will judge the type of caffeine a Professor brings into class."

stockfour/Shutterstock.com

6.   How Can Sociology Help the World? Real-World Jobs, How Sociology Can Take Place in All Careers

Now that you understand the research process, let's take a moment to understand how this can apply to the world outside of this class. As I have mentioned before, I know many of you will be going on to non-Sociological professions. However, thinking about things Sociologically can still help you. For example, if you are working in a workplace with a great deal of conflict, you can use your knowledge of Conflict theories to seek to understand where the division is, and how to fix it. You can look at a slow month at your business, and find that perhaps you should close earlier in the cold winter months. You will save money on operating costs, and only were able to spot this issue due to looking at the sales you had and when they were more frequent.

All people can benefit from understanding how to come up with a topic, and form it into a testable hypothesis. You will gain the respect of your colleagues if you can back up your beliefs

g-stockstudio/Shutterstock.com

with evidence. It helps to gain credibility to illustrate you understand the relationship between causation and correlation, and are not merely seeking to gain others on your side without first ensuring your points have a firm foundation.

Activity 3: Setting Up Your Experiment

In this activity you will: come up with a hypothesis, with a testable DV and IV. Decide what type of data you will collect.

STEP 1: First, come up with a Sociological topic. Write your topic here.

Jacob Lund/Shutterstock.com

STEP 2: Clearly identify your dependent and independent variable.

STEP 3: Next, you must decide if you will be collecting quantitative or qualitative data.

Activity 4: Inferring Causation from Correlation

In this activity you will set up an example of an experiment with an example of a flaw where you inferred causation when it is simply correlation.

Dean Drobot/Shutterstock.com

- What is the dependent variable?

- What is the independent variable?

- What is the correlation?

- What is the real causation? Think: what is really causing the change to occur?

- Why would someone confuse the real cause with thinking the DV was actually changing because of the IV?

- How can you change the experiment to eliminate this confusion? Most of the time this will involve making a more specific hypothesis.

CHAPTER 3
Socialization

1. Learning to Be "Civilized"
2. Socialization versus Brainwashing
3. Agents of Socialization: Family, School, Friends
4. Reality versus "Reality": Examples of How We Can Have Different Versions of Reality

1. Learning to Be "Civilized"

"*That's SO uncivilized!*" Wow, what an insult right?! We know that isn't something nice to say, we certainly don't want that said about us—but what does that even mean? From a Sociological perspective, we know that only the things which occur in the natural world would be considered "natural." Everything else? All of that would be man made. Culture is all made by humans, and therefore none of it is truly natural. It may feel that way, as the culture we have grown up with has become such a part of our lives, it can be subconscious at times.

2. Socialization versus Brainwashing

In fact, culture is all taught to us through a very specific process—**socialization**. To be socialized means to be taught the norms, values, behaviors, and so on of a distinct culture. Cultures vary across time periods and geographical locations, and the socialization that occurs will always be different. The common component of socialization is that every civilization socializes its members, though what they teach them can be highly different.

Think, for example, of the phrase from our modern day American culture—"man's best friend."

I am sure you knew right away what I am referring to—a dog is considered to be a man's best friend in our current culture. I am a self-professed "dog mom." of two adopted beagle Chihuahua mix dogs, Pumpkin and Pixie. I love spoiling my dogs, and think nothing of letting them up on the couch or bed to cuddle and spend time together. As

Nina Buday/Shutterstock.com

I have been socialized to consider dogs to be acceptable in the house as pets, this does not seem odd to others in my culture either. They have been socialized in the same way. However, there are other places in the world where having a dog inside the home would not be considered sanitary behavior. There are even places in the world where they are socialized to eat dogs, imagine how shocking this is compared to the socialization of our dog-loving culture!

Socialization occurs all throughout one's life. It never stops. Any time you are interacting with other people and the social world around you, you are allowing for potential socialization. When socialization becomes so severe, it enters into another category—brainwashing.

Socialization	Brainwashing

Some cultures purposefully brainwash their citizens. Think of a dictatorship, a society where it helps those in power to have others unwilling or unable to question their absolute authority. Think of settings where it is best for everyone to agree, where in order for the group as a whole to function, all members must act in accordance with the rules and law. A cult would be an example of a social group where brainwashing would occur. However, it does not take a cult or a dictatorship in order for some degree of brainwashing to be present. Perhaps we are all brainwashed into the norms of our society. Have you ever considered if you have been brainwashed at all?

3. Agents of Socialization: Family, School, Friends

When it comes to socialization, there are distinct areas of society one can study to see what sort of socialization is occurring. Different areas of your life have socialized you in different ways. These areas are known as the agents of socialization.

The first major agent of socialization is family.

Family impacts our socialization in huge ways. From the moment you are brought into this world, you depend upon your family for survival. Aside

Monkey Business Images/Shutterstock.com

from food and shelter, your family is also responsible to teach you life-threatening dangers for your own protection. This is layer one to the socialization. Your family will also teach you what you can and cannot do. Think of a young child getting punished, and not knowing that throwing a toy was the wrong thing to do. Through the punishment and the lessons the parents teach them, the child begins to have an understanding of which behaviors are acceptable or not. A family can socialize you to have a certain religion, or not have one at all. They can tell you that you can be anything you want to be when you grow up, or they can tell you they will only pay your college tuition if you study to become a brain surgeon. In a truly functional society, all families would have positive socialization results on their children. However, we know this is not always the case. Racism and sexism, for example, can be learned through the socialization of one's family.

The next agent of socialization is school.

Think of the school setting. Do you truly enjoy sitting silently, in an uncomfortable desk chair, with fluorescent lighting overhead, listening to your teachers talk? Maybe you shouldn't tell me your true answer there . . . All joking aside, it is important to realize the entire concept of our version of schooling is a product of socialization. Our culture highly values its school system and the

Rawpixel.com/Shutterstock.com

socialization you receive. How do I know this? Think of what is required of each member of our society. No matter what career you plan to have, we want you to complete our educational system. In fact, if you do not attend school there is a legal punishment for your parents! This may seem extreme, but realize that our society understands you are learning far more at school than just the academic concepts.

School teaches you how to interact with others. It teaches you that when in a group you can't suddenly blurt out ideas that come to you, you have to raise your hand and then wait patiently to either be called on, or not. You learn things like the golden rule, "do onto others as you would like them to do onto you." You hear stories about how the world operates, and you begin to form your own beliefs in a large part because of what you are hearing at school. Think of all the hours a day you spent in elementary school, then add on middle school, and then high school, and now even higher education. This is a lot of learning, and a lot of ability to be influenced by this agent of socialization.

In a functional society, there would be positive messages of empowerment in all schools, given to all children. However, we know this is not the case. Sadly, some teachers have biases toward students. They may tell students they are "bad" or "troublemakers." These encounters can socialize a student to internalize these messages. I have heard stories from students of their school telling them not to apply to certain colleges, that they will have no chance at getting in. Students have been told certain careers are outside the scope of what they should try to do, that they should aim for something "less challenging." If in fact we realize schools are having the ability to socialize the members of our society, we should seek to ensure positive messages and useful curriculum. It will come as no surprise to you that there is an entire area of Sociology dedicated to school and the social and cultural issues associated with schooling in our society.

The third area of socialization is friends. Your peers have a great deal of impact on your socialization process.

It isn't hard to come up with an example of a time your friends convinced you to do something, right? We have a term for this, known as peer pressure. Our peers have a great deal of impact on our lives. Perhaps you heard your parents tell you "if you lay down with dogs, you get up with fleas." This is a phrase people use to illustrate the concept that who you are friends with, who you are choosing to spend your time with, will have a large impact on your life.

During the school years of your life, you are around your friends a larger amount of your day than your own parents. You want to be liked, you want to fit in with your friends. Therefore you are willing to allow them to socialize you. At times, the socialization from your friends will be at odds with that

Jacob Lund/Shutterstock.com

of your parents. For example, your mom wants you to stay in and study for your upcoming test, and your friends want you to go to a party. Which one would you choose?

In a functional friendship, you would have positive socialization. Your parents probably want you to be friends with other students who work hard, get good grades, and are "good kids." Maybe this is not the same criteria you use when choosing friendships. It is important to consider the socialization messages youth are getting from their friends, and ensure peer pressure is not having a negative impact on those who might otherwise make better, wiser life decisions.

Note, there are many other agents of socialization. These are three of the main areas that impact us, and therefore are valuable to study when seeking an understanding of this concept. You will be asked to delve further into an analysis of your own socialization in one of our activities for this chapter.

4. Reality versus "Reality" Examples of How We Can Have Different Versions of Reality

The last topic we will consider for our discussion on socialization is the concept of reality. *There is not one true reality in an entire society, rather there is the dominant reality we are told to believe in, and then there are varying versions of "reality."* There are many examples you can use to illustrate this concept. Think of Bigfoot, of aliens, of a local favorite where I teach—the Jersey Devil. Perhaps these are just made up concepts, but to those who believe in them, those who say they have had personal encounters with them, is this not their own reality? In a functional society, all members would be able to agree on certain concepts. For example, if all members of a society agreed on the laws, you would not have a need for the enforcement of them. We know this isn't the case. Why would someone be willing to commit a crime, if they truly believed it is wrong to speed? Why would someone do so? The answer is that not everyone agrees with the reality of speeding being "wrong." Think of all of the concepts you have been told are untrue, all of the times you had an idea and were told "that's impossible!" Then take a moment to think of all of our big innovations, all of the technological inventions which only seemed impossible until they were done. Now you can realize—is there really one true version of reality? Or perhaps, is reality changing as we change, as we make new discoveries and advance in our society?

Activity 5: Agents of Socialization

- **STEP 1:** Pick one of the three agents of socialization we covered.
  List it here:

Dean Drobot/Shutterstock.com

- **STEP 2:** Next, come up with three examples from your life of the socialization you received from this agent of socialization.
  List them here:

    1.

    2.

    3.

- **STEP 3:** Finally, consider the socialization you received. Do you agree with what you were taught? Do you wish you had not been socialized to learn this? Do you feel this was brainwashing? Analyze each of your three examples here:

    1.

    2.

    3.

Activity 6: Reality Activity. Bigfoot, Aliens, Out of Body Experiences, and so on

- **STEP 1:** Pick an example of "reality," that is, pick a concept our mainstream culture does not agree is a real thing. For example, Bigfoot, Aliens, Out of body experiences, and so on.

    List it here:

aleks1949/Shutterstock.com

- **STEP 2:** Why does our culture not agree on this topic? What about it is unacceptable to our current reality?

    Explain here:

- **STEP 3:** What are your views on this topic? Is it in fact just a "reality" or is it truly reality? Should this concept be adopted by our dominate culture? Why or why not?

    Analyze here:

CHAPTER 4
Culture

1. Dominant American Culture. Describe and Give Examples

When someone refers to culture within our current-day society, what do they really mean? If they say something such as, "*Man, I really love our culture!*" you may find yourself wondering, what specific thing are they expressing love for? *Culture* is made up of everything man-made. All natural things, such as nature, animals, the weather, and so on, are not made by man. Then there is everything else; all art, music, food, clothing, language—all of that is culture. Culture is divided into two distinct categories: material and nonmaterial. *Material culture* is all of the tangible items, such as a cross for Christianity, a textbook for learning how great Sociology is, and a coffee cup for teaching fuel, of course. *Nonmaterial culture* is all culture that is not made up of tangible items. This includes thoughts, beliefs, values, judgments, and norms. All cultures have both material and nonmaterial culture.

Each society has a *mainstream culture*. This is the culture in which the majority of people participate, or the culture of those in power. Think of example in our current culture. Would sports be a part of mainstream American culture? I'd say yes.

Think of all of the things that align with sports in our culture, all of the evidence we have that shows us people value sports. We have the Super Bowl, a huge televised football event. We have all of the clothing, sports fans choose shirts and hats to show others which team they support. We have people purchasing tickets for sporting events, many of which are expensive. We have a tailgate culture, where fans get

Monkey Business Images/Shutterstock.com

together before games to eat and drink beer, and bond with each other. We could go on here. You can see that sports are a big part of our culture, whether or not you are a participant in them.

Other examples of mainstream culture can be seen in national holidays. You can tell what a culture values by seeing what holidays they are willing to give people off from work or school for. Think about it—in our culture most workplaces and schools give Christian holidays off, even if they are public schools or employers. We have a policy of separation of church and state, and yet if you examine our culture, you know that we still align with Christian calendar days. This is an example of how culture is not always logical or easy to understand, and in fact it can be difficult to understand other cultures at times.

Think of Christmas, and how not everyone who celebrates it it truly believes in Jesus or reads the Bible. They may never set foot into a church but may have a Christmas tree in their home. You can imagine how someone outside of our culture would be confused. They might say, "Oh I see you have a tree up, you must be Christian." And what if you were to respond, "Oh no, I just like the idea behind the tree. I don't agree with the religious

Yuganov Konstantin/Shutterstock.com

part at all." The outsider might be confused, and there is a perfect illustration of how complex culture can be!

2. Subcultures and Countercultures, and the Difference between Them

Subcultures are a smaller type of culture, which form off of the dominate one. Subcultures do not have to conflict with the dominate culture. If a subculture directly disagrees with or conflicts with the dominant culture there is another term for it, it is a *counterculture*. An example of a subculture would be your friend group. You form your own culture, you have your own ideas about what is fun, and you have your own informal rules about what it means to be a good friend. If your

golubovystock/Shutterstock.com

friend group happens to be a gang, then you would find yourself in not only a subculture, but a counterculture as well.

The relationship between subculture and counterculture can be confusing, so here is the best way to break it down: all countercultures are subcultures. Not all subcultures are countercultures. Confused yet? Let's walk through more examples.

Think of the music you listen to. There are so many different music genres out there. You may like music from various genres, but let's say there is one in particular you prefer. If you mostly listen to rap

music, that is a subculture. You may not align with the lyrics, but you are listening to them. You may even rap along, but you may not fully agree with what the lyrics are telling you to do. Even though you may not personally dress like the rappers you listen to, you can see there are fashion trends.

This would sharply contrast with the country music subculture.

Country music artists most likely dress very different from rap artists. If you went to a country music

Gordo25/Shutterstock.com

concert, I bet you could tell by looking at the crowd that it is not a rap concert, even if no one told you who was performing that night. The lyrics in country music would also speak of different experiences and describe life in a different way from rap music. The differences in the music are in part due to the differences in life experiences of the artists. Music fans often choose music to listen to based on what resonates with them, what they can relate to. Each genre then ends up forming its own subculture, based on the people who listen to it, the artists who make the music in the genre, and the experiences expressed in the lyrics.

3.   Culture Varies Geographically and by Time

You now know that culture is man-made. It is comprised of material and nonmaterial culture. There is a dominate culture in a society, and there are also subcultures. Some subcultures are countercultures, meaning they run counter to the dominant culture, they oppose it in some way. The next piece of the cultural puzzle to understand is the fact that culture changes, it does not stay the same. Due to the fact that culture is created by humans, as humans change and evolve, so does the culture. There are two key facts to keep in mind when examining culture: the historical aspect and the geographical aspect. It is helpful to break this down using examples, so let's start with *Historical culture.*

Think of the United States of America. If you were to say, "Women are equals in our culture. Women have the right to vote and they have the right to own property and work outside the home, the same as men." Right away, you may have many people agree with you. You may then jump to the conclusion of saying, "The US culture has always had gender equality, and women have always had equal rights." However, this would be a mistake. You failed to remember the historical component to culture.

Everett Historical/Shutterstock.com

In fact, the reality in our culture is that women had to fight hard for their rights. Women were not easily given the right to vote, rather they had to fight for it. You can look at various historical times and see that the rights and treatment of women vary greatly, and that is all even within our same culture, the same location. This leads into the next important piece when examining culture.

All culture is *Geographical culture.* Different people who live in different places have different cultures. You can compare countries and see differences: different languages, different styles, different occupations and industries. You can also compare various locations within one country. Think of within the United States. There are different regions known for their distinct cultures. The culture of the Southern United States is not the same as the West Coast of the country. If you have ever moved within the country you would really understand this firsthand. However, even if you have simply traveled within the country, you can see how different cultures can be, sometimes even hours apart.

Think of accents as an example of this concept. I went to law school in West Virginia, and I grew up outside Washington, DC. These locations are within the same country, and only a few hours away. However, when I moved to West Virginia I very quickly realized their way of pronouncing words was very different from my own. This lead me to describe their way of speaking as having an accent. On their end, they could say the same about me. It was due to my personal perspective that I considered my way as the default way of speaking and theirs as different. This is all part of geographical culture.

Within geographical culture, you can also have very different norms and laws based in different places. You run the risk as a traveler of not knowing the local culture and potentially offending the locals. On the extreme end of that spectrum you also run the risk of not knowing the laws and committing a crime without being aware. Within our own country we now have different laws on the usage of marijuana, for example. If you are coming from Colorado where you are legally permitted to engage in the use of this drug and you travel to New Jersey, where it is currently illegal, you could get arrested. You might say, "I didn't realize this was illegal here! It's legal where I live." That won't be an acceptable excuse, as the culture is tied with the laws, and you are held to the standard of obeying the laws wherever you are geographically.

Shutterstock.com

4. Ethnocentric

If you are so deeply tied to your own culture you run the risk of being *ethnocentric*. This term is not a compliment, it is not something you would want to be called. Being ethnocentric means you are looking at other cultures and judging them against your own. You are not judging cultures neutrally, as a Sociologist would, but rather you are comparing them in terms of better or worse. You would say, "Your culture is dif-

Lipik Stock Media/Shutterstock.com

ferent than mine, and therefore I don't like it." An example of being ethnocentric would be if you were to travel somewhere else and eat the food the locals eat. You would then say, "This is gross! I wish they had the food my mom makes me. That is so much better." You are being ethnocentric. Perhaps you wish you could have a cheeseburger, but if you went to my house, you'd only find a veggie burger, no meat here. You might say that isn't "real food," I have heard that before. That is being ethnocentric. You are also missing out on the delicious and healthy options of a vegan diet, but hey, I'll have to write more on that in my next book.

5. Culture Shock

Culture Shock is what can happen if you are being ethnocentric. When you are introduced to another culture that is different from your own, if you are so tightly tied to your culture being right, you will view the other culture as wrong. This will be an unpleasant experience—culture shock is not fun. An example of culture shock would be if you travel to another country and they do not have a certain fast-food option you are used to. You would say "I can't get the food I want? I am so mad!"

Anatoliy Karlyuk/Shutterstock.com

You are shocked, you assumed everywhere in the world has the same options as your home-town. Perhaps they have even better options available, but because you were so tied to your idea of what a good option would be, you could not even appreciate the different offerings. When culture shock happens you can feel anxious, stressed, and angry. You can attempt to insist others change to be more like your own culture, as a way to resolve the uncomfortable feelings. This type of behavior would lead to a very boring world, with only one culture possible, and no variance allowed. Variety is the spice of life, and an appreciation for other cultures is a much more fun way to live than living with culture shock.

6. Cultural Relativism

Cultural Relativism is a better solution to dealing with cultures. Instead of judging cultures against your own, you can look at them on their own. You can still admit there are differences in cultures, without having to view them as better or worse. Cultural relativism is help-ful when examining cultures. If you start from a judgmental place, you will often be unable to get past that, and cannot delve further into an analysis. Instead, if you apply cul-tural relativism, you can begin to

KIRAYONAK YULIA/Shutterstock.com

understand where others are coming from. Perhaps the culture is different from your own, but you learn something you like from it, and can apply that to your own life.

I remember studying French in high school. I was learning the language, that is what the course and credit were for. However, I also began to develop a love for the culture. We watched films in class to help hear the conversations, and I found myself drawn to the clothing styles and decor in the films as well. I was appreciating the differences and learning about culture beyond my own. It enriches your life when you can apply cultural relativism to the world around you. You can infuse the best from each culture into your own life, and create the life that best aligns with your interests and values.

Activity 7: Subculture You Are a Part of

- Think of three examples of subcultures you are a part of.

golubovystock/Shutterstock.com

- List them here:

- Pick the best one, and analyze.

- What behavior is required of you as a member of this subculture?

- What norms are parts of this subculture?

- Is this subculture a counterculture? Why or why not?

- Is there anything you disagree with about this subculture? Explain.

Activity 8: Think of a Time in Your Life You Experienced Culture Shock. Describe

- When have you experienced culture shock? Explain the details.

- Where were you? Who were you with? What shocked you?

- Consider your thoughts toward the situation. Were you being ethnocentric?

DarkBird/Shutterstock.com

- Were there any negative impacts from your reaction?

- How could you have better handled the situation?

- What did you learn from the situation, about yourself and about the world?

CHAPTER 5
Structure

1. Explaining Structures in Society: Social Institutions, Legal Structure, Health Care, and So On
2. Explain How We Have Various Roles and Norms in Different Structures: Legal Structures, Health Care System
3. Roles, Role Conflict, Role Strain
4. Values and Beliefs

Now that you have the basic framework for Sociology—understanding how it is a social science, what we study, how we study things, and how socialization works—we are moving on to another area of society: Structure. The three main components of Sociology are culture, structure, and power. We learned about culture in Chapter 4, and now we will learn the structural layer. In Chapter 6, we will get the complete understanding by examining power.

1.   Explaining Structures in Society: Social Institutions, Legal Structure, Health Care, and So On

In order to best understand *structure*, it helps to start with an example. You can really think of any large part of society that helps to hold things together. Without any structures in society, we would have total anarchy. There would be no government, no money, no laws, and no social norms—life would look very different from how it does for us now.

The first type of structure to consider is *social institutions*. These are the areas of life where we have made divisions based on social reasons. Think of all the groups of friends out there in the world. They may not have formal rules or laws binding them together, but they certainly have some sort of organization. Structures can have formal or informal organization. Friends' groups are formed informally, and people pick who to hang out with based on a variety of reasons. If you enjoy someone's company, you choose to be around them. If they do something you no longer like, that relationship may end. Friendships are structured, and they help structure your social life.

You can join clubs or groups, to have a more formal social institution structure in your life. Some of these groups even require money to join, in the form of dues. Think of Greek life on campus.

It costs money to join a fraternity. You would pick the fraternity that most closely aligns with your interests, and hope that they pick you back. If that ends up happening the next step requires you to pay money. The structure there is that you will have to obey the rules of the fraternity in order to keep in good standing. If not, you run the risk of disobeying the structure and getting kicked out. In order for the group to keep functioning they need you to stay in line with the rules. A fraternity could not exist if the members did not respect the structure of the social institution.

The next type of structures you can consider are *legal structures*. Remember how we just learned about social institutions? Well, let's say you fall in love with someone. That is a pretty social process, right? Spending time together, going on dates, getting to know one another, all of that would be involved in the social arena. However, once you decide to take the big leap into our legally binding institution of marriage, this becomes part of our legal structure.

Marriage is not the same as dating. In order to end a relationship, you merely need to breakup. To end a marriage? You have to go through a legal process of a divorce in

nd3000/Shutterstock.com

Vadim Rodnev/Shutterstock.com

KirylV/Shutterstock.com

our society to formally end the legally binding contract of marriage. We have legal protections in our society to decide how to end a marriage—who gets what property, how can you change your name back to your maiden name, how to decide on custody matters, and so on. All of this is part of our legal structure.

Aside from marriage, we have many other laws and rules holding our society together. Think of the consequences for breaking a law.

It could result in simply a warning, or

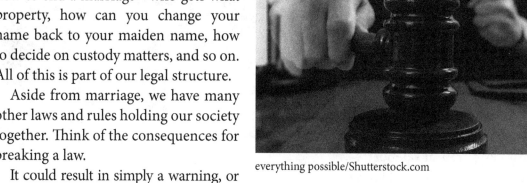

everything possible/Shutterstock.com

it could result in a ticket, a small fine. If the law you break is a serious offense, you can find yourself getting arrested and charged with a crime. Being in jail, getting a criminal record—all of these things are put in place as part of our legal structure to deter people from wanting to be criminals. Can you imagine what our society would be like if there were not laws holding people in place? Some theorize man would be inherently good without laws, but many people fear such a world. What do you think life would be like without the legal structure?

The next structure of our society to consider is our *Health Care System*. We have a structure in place in our society where people must pay for health care insurance if they want it. We did not decide, like some other countries have done, that health care is a universal right. Rather, in our society we view it to be something people must earn. When you do get sick, where do you go? You know to go to either a doctor's office or a hospital, right? Remember that this is not natural, not all societies throughout history have had a formal medical system exactly like ours.

We deem what medical treatments we view as "real." There are certain procedures, such as treatments for cancer where we assume the Western medical way is the only way. Chemotherapy can be seen as the only option. There might be other medical options that would work as well, such as massage therapy or acupuncture. However, if in our medical system we do not respect the treatments, our health care structure will not pay for them. This helps to illustrate that there

Monkey Business Images/Shutterstock.com

are in fact cultural components to our health care structure.

When looking at the various structures in society, the type of theories Sociologists usually use is known as *Structural Functionalist Theory*. Here is an example of a Functionalist theory. If you were looking at our legal system and saying, "Why do we have so many people commit a crime and then go on to commit another crime? Why do we have such high rates of repeat offenders?" If our system was working well, if the legal

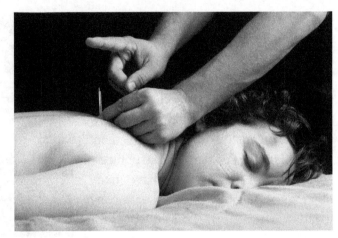

Doglikehorse/Shutterstock.com

structure was functioning, we would not see these rates being so high. You can look at this from a structural functionalist perspective, and say "Is the structure functioning?" If, as often times is the case, you find the structure is not functioning, then you can examine further, and seek to understand why there is a problem.

2. Explain How We Have Various Roles and Norms in Different Structures: Legal Structures, Health Care System

It is important, now that you know a few of the examples of different structures, to understand how they impact us on a personal level. Think of any main structure in your life. Let's use one you are engaged in right now, the structure of college education. Within this structure, you know you have to do certain things in order to succeed. If you want to be a good student, this can be measured by getting good grades. In order to get those good grades, you know you have to engage in certain behaviors and not engage in others. Good class attendance would be likely

to lead to a good grade, whereas standing up in the middle of class and yelling out, "This class sucks!" would probably not be the best idea. You learn to behave in certain ways depending on the specific structure you are taking part in.

Within your life, in each day, you will have to switch your roles and behaviors depending on which structure you are currently in. So, you may wake up as a child if you still live with your parents. That means you have to obey the family

LStockStudio/Shutterstock.com

structure and obey the rules of your parents, who own the home if you want to stay living in it. Then you attend class, and have to obey all of the structures of the school. Within your class schedule you have different teachers, and each one may have their own rules for their specific class. After school you go to work and while there you have to obey the structures of the workplace. If you do not obey the rules and do your work as it is assigned to you, you can get fired, and lose the right to take part in that structure. After work you may go and spend some time with your friends, and take part in that social structure. All in one day's time, all for one person, many different structures are taking place and impacting your life.

3.   Roles, Role Conflict, Role Strain

We discussed roles, as we said you have different roles in different structures. *Roles* are the expected behaviors depending on each setting. It can be difficult to partake in all of the roles in your life at one time, as they often have different and conflicting expectations. Think of the *role strain* you can feel from being a student, employee, good friend, and significant other. It is a challenge to balance all of the roles, and do so in a successful way. If you have too many roles that are not in alignment you can suffer from a total *role conflict* and you will have to leave some roles behind. Juggling roles is what leads to stress in our lives, and most people would admit they are currently juggling many different opposing roles.

ESB Professional/Shutterstock.com

Norms are the expectations society puts on us. Our culture has ideas about the way we are supposed to act. Yes, there are laws, the legal rules. And there are also social rules, those are the norms of our society. You are not supposed to wear a bathing suit to class, right? But if you wore what you are supposed to wear to class to the pool, that wouldn't be good either. You know all of this, it has been so socialized into you that you don't even have to consciously say "Don't wear a swimsuit to class." You won't find that rule on the syllabus for this course. That is how easy it is to know the norms. The difficult part about norms? When you are exposed to other cultures, other structures you are not used to, there is no way to know the norms. You are likely to use your own system of norms as your default setting, and can sometimes break the norms of other settings without knowing it.

g-stockstudio/Shutterstock.com

4.   Values and Beliefs

The last part to the structure puzzle is understanding *values*. When you study a culture, you can easily observe its laws and norms. Beyond what you are observing, what is really being reflected is what the culture *believes* in. You can tell a culture's values and beliefs by seeing what actions the culture allows. Not every culture believes that women are equal to men. If you observe the laws and norms in those types of cultures, you may find places where women cannot drive cars, where they cannot vote, or own their own property. This would differ from the structure in our society. We have values and beliefs around the way women should be treated, which then impacts the laws and norms we have.

Another example you can use is the idea of drugs. Our culture has made certain judgment calls about what drugs are okay for legal consumption. Many people disagree with the fact that marijuana is deemed illegal. They have a different belief in the purpose of this plant from what our government believes. Does this make the government's belief the right one? Now you can see how values and beliefs can get complex. Within the same society, within the same structure, you will find various belief systems. Most people seek out like-minded friends, whose values and beliefs most closely align with their own. This makes the structure of their social lives more enjoyable.

patronestaff/Shutterstock.com

Activity 9: Social Institution and Structure

List three social institutions:

1.

2.

3.

Pick one of the social institutions. Describe the structure of it—what is the culture, what are the norms, what are the rules, laws, and so on.

Why would someone want to join this particular social institution?

Activity 10: Roles

List and describe the various roles you have in your life. Make sure you have at least five.

Where do you have role strain? Why do you have a strain?

Where do you have role conflict? Why do you have role conflict?

What roles will you likely have to give up, as a result of role strain or conflict? Why?

CHAPTER 6
Power

1. Power versus Power Over
2. Different Kinds of Power—Not Just about Physical Force/Coercion, Also Ideology
3. Money and Power

The three main Sociological lenses are Culture, Structure, and Power. We now find ourselves analyzing the last of the three—*Power*. Power is a huge Sociological concept. The truth is, it would be almost impossible to analyze any issue from a Sociological perspective without considering the power dynamics. Power is expressed in many ways, but the easiest way to think about it is one's ability to get their way, regardless of the desires of others. When you consider power structures in society, you quickly realize the

KieferPix/Shutterstock.com

more fun position—being the one with the power. Therefore, you can understand that in order for people to give their power away to someone else, something pretty significant must be happening. We will use examples to understand the different strategies people use to obtain power. First, it is vital to understand the basic relationship inherent in power situations.

1.   Power versus Power Over

Power over is a concept which helps us to get the total picture of what is going on. It is never totally about who has the power, you always have to consider an additional part—who do they have the power over? Remember what I said before—it is not common for someone to want to willingly give their power away. For example, do you like it when people tell you what to do? Do you like having to sit quietly and listen while someone else lectures you? You do so in your college classes, right? But of course, you know it is all leading somewhere—first a good grade, and then hopefully to a diploma. It would be a totally different story if you showed up twice a week to listen to your professor lecture you about a subject, devoid of any benefit to you. I just can't see that happening, can you?

Matej Kastelic/Shutterstock.com

The truth is, when someone has power they always have power over someone else. Think of your parents. They have innate power over you from birth. You literally cannot survive as a baby unless your parents provide for you in the form of food and shelter.

Your boss has power over you, in the sense that they are determining if you keep your job or not, if you get paid each pay period or not. You know they have power over you, and you allow it because you need money

Joana Lopes/Shutterstock.com

to survive in this world. You are willing to give someone power over you if in some way it makes logical sense. You are willing to give the professor the power over you to talk and test you on what they say, and eventually determine your final grade which will go on your grade point average (GPA). It makes sense to you, because you understand this will pay off in the long run, as you move on with your career and professional aspirations.

But what happens in cases where someone wants power over you and you don't want to give it to them? This brings us to our next section.

2.   Different Kinds of Power—Not Just about Physical Force/Coercion, Also Ideology

If someone wants power over you, and logically you don't want to give it, what happens? The individual will try to get the power from you in one of two distinct ways.

Coercion versus Ideology are the two ways one can approach gaining power. Coercion in its simplest form can be described as using physical force or the threat of physical force to get someone to do something. Yes, that sounds a bit vague, but let's walk through a couple examples to help explain.

Mark Agnor/Shutterstock.com

If, for example, someone were to walk up to you, as a stranger, and simply say, "Hey, give me your money," would you do it? I am guessing no, right? But what if the same person were to walk up with you and say the exact same words, but the only difference is that they had a gun in their hand, and pointed it at you? Would you be more willing to give your money to this person? I'd guess yes.

The threat of violence can be used to enforce social control in a society. Compliance of the masses can be created through police enforcement. Think about a protest. We have the right in our society to participate in peaceful protest.

Even without those present at a protest becoming violent, police will be present. This is to enforce the peaceful compliance. The threat of police is there to keep people in line. If, for some reason, the protesters choose to become violent, the police will then

Wade Jackman/Shutterstock.com

use force to utilize coercion. They may use their Taser or spray them with pepper spray to contain them.

You can see how in the moment coercion can be extremely effective. It does not involve much effort for the person doing the act either. If you have a weapon or the upper hand by way of physical force, you can easily get people to listen to you. However, the drawback to this strategy is that it is not a long lasting form of power. The moment you withdraw the coercion, that is to say the moment you no longer have the weapon, the power is gone as well. In fact, people become resentful over controlling figures. Think of prisoners and their stories of how they sometimes riot against the guards. We know it is human nature to not feel good when someone is using physical force or the threat of physical force to gain power over us.

Skyward Kick Productions/Shutterstock.com

Ideology, on the other hand, is all about changing someone's mind. This tactic involves a great deal of effort on the part of the person doing the persuading. They must develop a convincing argument and present it in a way that actually changes your mind. This takes much more effort in the beginning, however, it is a much longer lasting form of power. Think of a debate. If during a debate with someone you started out having totally opposing

doomu/Shutterstock.com

views, but then during the debate you listened to what they said, and actually found yourself agreeing with them, they changed your ideology. We know this is not an easy task. People tend to be very connected to their own belief systems, especially ones that they hold very close, such as religion or politics.

The big key to remember is: when you can convince someone to change their mind on something that is a much longer lasting form of power.

3.   Money and Power

Money and Power are very closely related in our society. In fact, I am sure you have even heard people make the statement that "money equals power." For that reason, it would be incomplete to explain the Sociological concept of power without including its connection to money. Many people in our society never even stop to think about what money is. Think now—take out a dollar. Look at it up close. What is it really? Literally—it is a piece of paper. We have assigned this piece of paper a very crucial meaning, it is the form of our currency that we recognize.

The piece of paper itself is not what has the value. The value is something we as a society give to the paper. We give money so much value, in fact, that it is very difficult to think of anything else we value as much. With this high value, comes a sense of power given to money as well. Those who have lots of money have power and influence in our society. There are very few things that cannot be bought. Many people complain about how even people can have a "price," meaning there are things many would not do, but when a monetary reward is given, they will change their stance. In the most dramatic sense, we even have people willing to kill other people for a certain price. Ever hear of a hit man?

Masson/Shutterstock.com

You can see the way money is seen as power in many ways in our society. Think of many song lyrics. Songs talk about how cool someone is with a lot of money. Music videos depict the type of lifestyle one can have with money. Professional athletes and movie stars show off their homes and expensive clothing on social media, the list goes on and on . . . It is important to understand

ESB Professional/Shutterstock.com

when you are analyzing power in society from a Sociological perspective, money will play a huge role. Most people would like more money, how do you feel about money and the sense of power you currently have?

Activity 11: Power

Describe a time in your life when you had power.

gotogestoeber/Shutterstock.com

How did you gain the power?

Did you abuse the power at all?

What did the power position feel like?

Activity 12: Power Over

Describe a time in your life where someone has had power over you.

VGstockstudio/Shutterstock.com

How did the individual gain power over you?

What did it feel like to not have the power?

CHAPTER 7
Norms and Laws

1. Norms versus Laws: Norms Are Social Codes of Conduct; Laws Are Legal Ones
2. How They Regulate Behavior in Our World
3. There Are Punishments for Breaking Both

Norms and laws are critical to the regulation of the social world. Therefore, they are very important in the field of Sociology. Imagine a world with no norms, no laws, nothing governing it. Freaked out? Most people would be. Hence why we have become so attached to our norms and laws.

WAYHOME studio/Shutterstock.com

1.   Norms versus Laws: Norms Are Social Codes of Conduct; Laws Are Legal Ones

Norms are the social code of conduct within a culture.

Laws are the legal code of conduct within a culture.

Each of they regulate the world around us. Here is the key to their relationship to remember:

Breaking a norm can break a law. Breaking a law can break a norm. There are some laws you can break that don't break a norm. There are some norms you can break that don't break a law.

Confused yet? Let's get some examples to help.

To start, let's walk through an example of a norm and how it would be broken.

Basic Breaking a Norm Example

Let's say you want to have a conversation with a stranger. You might want to keep it short and sweet, right? You can just say "Hi, how are you?" In response, the stranger can operate within the existing norm. If the stranger chooses to say, "Fine, thank you," then all is well, no worries. However, the stranger can step outside the box of socially acceptable conduct, and break a norm in how they choose to respond. What, if instead of saying the usual chitchat, the stranger says "Oh man! I have been waiting all day for someone to ask me. In fact, I have so much to tell you . . ." And then proceeds to fill you in on the intimate details of their life? I am guessing you might not be all that happy.

Handshake versus Fist Bump Example

Another example of how norms can play out in the social world can be seen in how you greet someone. If you are meeting a professional contact for the first time, let's

Dean Drobot/Shutterstock.com

Mooshny/Shutterstock.com

say you are interviewing for a job—you better be very careful how you go to greet them. Would you go in for a "first bump" I would not suggest that unless you are in a very informal work culture. In fact, refusing a handshake can totally ruin a first impression in some business settings. However, after you are done with your interview if you go to hang out with your friends and you attempt to greet them with a formal handshake, will they think it is odd? This illustrates norms. We know where to do certain behaviors. We

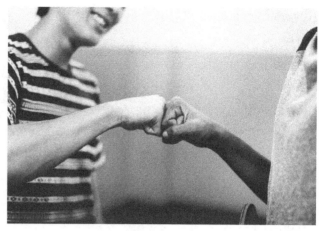

Rawpixel.com/Shutterstock.com

have been socialized to act certain ways in certain settings. If you get the setting wrong, you do the wrong behavior in the wrong setting, you are breaking a norm. This illustrates that the same exact behavior can be fine, and even encouraged in some settings, while it would be totally inappropriate in others. I am sure you can think of many other examples.

Breaking a Norm That Breaks a Law Example

The next piece of the puzzle is how you can break a norm that also breaks a law. Laws are more formal than norms. You can get arrested and thrown into jail for refusing to follow the laws. If you break a norm perhaps your only punishment will be a mean look. But when you break a norm that also breaks a law? Now you are in real trouble.

Think of the values in our culture. The ones we hold dearest are the ones which are most strongly enforced when it comes to the laws. You can't be violent toward others, you can't steal, and you certainly can't kill. All of those would be laws that are broken, yes. It also breaks a norm to physically hurt another person. If you were to witness someone walk up and punch a random stranger, you would not only think that they were guilty of committing a crime, but you would make judgements about their character as well. When people do something that is outside of the normally expected behavior and it is also illegal, they are breaking both a norm and a law.

Evannovostro/Shutterstock.com

Breaking a Law That Does Not Break a Norm Example

Kzenon/Shutterstock.com

Now, things start to get a little trickier when you try to come up with examples for the following category—behaviors that break a law that do not break a norm. Your initial response might be, "But wouldn't any lawless behavior be breaking a norm?" Not exactly.

Here is the example I always give my students. What if I were to come into class late, and as I came in I told you, "I am so sorry I am late, I was speeding on the way over and got a ticket." Speeding is illegal. Everyone knows you should drive the speed limit, and if you do so you will avoid getting a speeding ticket. Shouldn't I be judged as breaking a norm for this behavior? Not really. Most people have driven over the speed limit at some point in their lives. Often times when someone is caught speeding, the reaction is empathy for them for getting caught, rather than judgment for the behavior. So right there you have an example of breaking the law without breaking a norm. If on the other hand, I was speeding on the way to class, but it was in a school zone and I hit a child, that would then break a norm, and be seen as offensive by most students. Do you understand the difference?

2.   How They Regulate Behavior in Our World

So how do norms and laws regulate the behavior of people? Well, the most important thing to realize is that most people like to be liked. Think about this, you might say "I don't care what other people think." But would you really want to live in a society where you were a total outcast? Most people would not be happy about that. Social connections are important to our mental and emotional health. Those who break norms run the risk of punishment and so do those who break laws.

3.   There Are Punishments for Breaking Both

Social punishments are the punishments for breaking norms.
   Legal punishments are the punishments for breaking laws.

Neither are fun or enjoyable, in most cases. There are times, however, when people want to break a norm or a law. Some people want to stand out from the crowd, some even enjoy negative attention. Other times it is vital to break a law to make a public point.

Why do we need punishments? Social order rests on people behaving. It isn't a given in society that people will do as they are told. There must be measures in place to keep the order going. Think about this—if tomorrow everyone woke up and decided they no longer wanted to wear shoes, what would happen? Humans are not born with shoes on. Shoes are a piece of culture, they are an article of clothing that our society has decided is necessary for living. Not every society throughout history has insisted on wearing shoes. If you tried to adopt this new shoeless philosophy and went into work barefoot, I don't imagine it would go very well. That is, unless you were a lifeguard.

Evgeniy Kalinovskiy/Shutterstock.com

Activity 13: Breaking a Norm

Describe a time you broke a norm.

KlaraBstock/Shutterstock.com

What was the social reaction?

How did you feel?

Will this reaction stop you from breaking this norm in the future?

Why or why not?

Activity 14: Breaking a Law

Pick a crime.

Mehaniq/Shutterstock.com

Describe how someone could break it.

Why would someone commit this crime?

How can we prevent this crime in our society?

CHAPTER 8
Media and Social Media

1. Social Media versus Traditional Media
2. Types of Media: Memes, Facebook, Instagram, Televised News
3. Different Versions of the Same "Truth"
4. The Looking-Glass Self

1. Social Media versus Traditional Media

If you were to say "media" to a crowd of people, you might get a very different reaction from them, depending on their age. It is safe to say we live in a world with many types of media. Social media is such a vital part of our media system now, that it would be impossible to conduct a Sociological analysis of media without including it. One's age would be likely to determine if they would consider social media to be a valid form of media. You have to remember, there are some people who did not experience the presence of social media until well into adulthood. Others grew up their entire lives with social media. Once you understand this key difference it is easy to see how people may view the validity of social media very differently.

There is a lot of debate in our current culture, as to what constitutes "reputable media." That is to say, is traditional media the only form of media that can be trusted? Perhaps

Rawpixel.com/Shutterstock.com

63

reading the newspaper or watching the nightly news should be respected over obtaining information from Twitter or Facebook? Sociologists would caution against using such black and white terms. There are important things to be gained from all forms of media, traditional or social. We will walk through a few examples of types of media to understand how they impact our lives.

motttive/Shutterstock.com

2. Types of Media: Memes, Facebook, Instagram, Televised News

Memes are one of my favorite types of media to study. Think about who creates memes? Individual people! Anyone can create a meme, as long as you have access to images and text, right? And how do memes become popular? When people relate to a meme and share it, it is spread through social media. A meme is a piece of media containing an image and text, and it says something about society. Think about it. The most popular memes are ones a lot of people can relate to. They may contain images from shows many people watched growing up, or they may show a famous person. The text is an additional layer that usually says something humorous.

The people reading it can connect with the message, and if they like it they might tag their friends so they can see it. If they really like the meme, and strongly feel a connection to the message, they may even share the meme. This is the way the meme picks up steam, and can even go "viral." When a piece of social media goes viral that means it gains attention on a large scale. Think of the popular memes you have seen again and again. What do they have in common? Most make

Uber Images/Shutterstock.com

you laugh and connect them to your own life. This is why memes are a vital new form of social media.

Facebook is a Popular Social Media Platform

Through Facebook, you can connect with people all over the world. What is unique about Facebook is the idea that "friends" don't have to be in person. This is what set Facebook apart when it was originally created. The spread of social

tuthelens/Shutterstock.com

media has led to a more global view of our world. This means we can see beyond our own location and interact with those all over the world. It enriches our lives in many ways. There are some criticisms of Facebook as a form of media. There is no way to know if the news you are reading on Facebook is based on facts, for example. People can spread misinformation by sharing links, and not realize the links they are sharing are full of untrue details. There was a lot of worry that stemmed from the most recent election, and talk about if other countries can utilize a platform such a Facebook to impact our election here in the United States.

Another interesting thing Facebook has done for our society is introduce the idea of "likes" into our culture. You know you have the ability to press a button and show you like something on Facebook. This is a form of instant gratification for the poster. They can see how many likes they get on a specific post, and measure if other people enjoy it or not. This could be seen in a positive light, if the person enjoys the attention they are getting. However, what happens when the likes go away? We have seen examples of Internet bullying on platforms such as Facebook. It is easy to hide behind a computer screen. We have also seen the creation of "catfishing," a term which refers to using the images of another person in order to deceive people. When you open up to the online world there are many positives that can be achieved with greater connection, though one needs to be aware of the potential dangers as well.

Instagram is a Popular Social Network Application That Features Photos

Users upload images to their account and they follow other users. You can comment and like the images others share, and there are business accounts as well. Instagram has options for going live, providing a video feed to your followers. This form of social media has many positives. Many state how inspiring this app is on a creative level. The networking possibilities are very conducive for small business owners, who can showcase

tanuha2001/Shutterstock.com

their products to followers without having to worry about paying advertising fees.

There are some complaints about Instagram. Business owners have complained that less people see their posts than they used to, a push they claim relates to Instagram's desire to have people pay to boost their posts, and get more visibility. There is also debate over nudity on the app, if it should be allowed, and if so, how much. Catfishing

SkillUp/Shutterstock.com

can occur on this platform as well. As with all forms of social media, users should be cautious with sharing personal details. There have been cases of people sharing they are going away on vacation, only to have them return to an empty home. Someone saw they were gone and robbed their home. Practicing responsible social media usage is a must in our new social media age.

Televised News is a Traditional Form of Media

There are many news stations, some of which play solely news reports, 24 hours a day. If you want to find televised news, any time of day, any day of the week, you certainly can. Prior to social media, televised news was a great way to obtain news in a timely manner. The newspaper would take a day to post, and some newspapers are published weekly. The nightly news became a way for people to obtain the biggest stories of each day, and it soon became a habit in many people's lives. The spread of social media has not replaced televised news.

The main complaint with televised news is the slants different channels take. Certain channels are known for being oriented with one political party, whereas other channels align more closely with another. Some worry news channels have become biased to the point they can no longer be trusted. Is there such a thing as totally unbiased, neutral news? The answer is no, and in the next section we will gain a greater understanding why.

3. Different Versions of the Same "Truth"

One of the issues of creditability when it comes to media is figuring out which form of media is bringing forth the truth. Yes, there are certain facts when an event occurs. For example, when a car accident occurs you can find out the exact location, the time of day, and the names of people involved. But beyond those core facts, that is where human interpretation comes in.

Who is to blame for the accident? Well, you might get a different story depending on who you ask, right? Now apply that same idea to something political that happens in the world. Who is right, who has the correct political stance on an issue? Well, that might depend on the source of news you are consuming, right?

tommaso79/Shutterstock.com

Understand that a Sociological opinion on news and media in general would be that it is all different versions. If you have one incident occurring you will end up with "different versions of the same truth." It is up to you as the consumer to be aware. You should never use any form of media without filtering it through your own best judgment. You know we live in a very media-oriented culture. Now it is up to you to become empowered by that fact, rather than becoming a victim of it.

4. The Looking-Glass Self

The looking-glass self is a concept that relates to media and our consumption of media. You can suffer the consequences of allowing our media to tell you what to think. This is dangerous enough when it deals with external topics. But what about when the media is impacting your views on your own self? We can see people begin to believe what others tell them about themselves. For example, if you got a lot of likes every time you posted a picture in a bikini, you might be more inclined to start posting only pictures in bikinis. After a long period of time, you could begin to associate your inherent worth with how you look in a bathing suit. On the other hand, if you get told you are unattractive all the time when you post pictures of yourself on social media, perhaps you will stop posting any pictures of yourself. You might delete your social media accounts entirely, depending on how bad you feel.

We know social media is available in our culture for people of any age. There is no age limit, if parents allow their children to join apps, they can join them. Some children even join apps without parental consent. You can imagine it could be especially harmful for children to participate in social media at times when they are particularly impressionable. There are Sociologists monitoring the impact of social media usage on society, and I am sure there will be much more to come as we move forward in our media and social media age.

Activity 15: Social Media

Describe your daily social media use.

sondem/Shutterstock.com

What apps do you use?

How much time a day do you spend on social media?

In what ways does social media impact your daily life?

How would you feel if you could no longer use social media?

Activity 16: Memes

Pick a meme you have seen.

Describe the meme—what is the image, what is the text saying?

Analyze the meme Sociologically. What does this meme say about society?

If you were to create your own meme, what would you create? What image would you use and what text would you write?

What does your meme say about society?

What does your meme say about yourself?

CHAPTER 9
Race and Ethnicity

1. What Is Race? What Is Ethnicity? Everyone Has an Ethnicity, and You Don't Just Say American
2. Culture and Ethnicity
3. Racism, Stereotypes, and Why They Are Hard to Get Rid of
4. Religion
5. Societal Progress

1. What Is Race? What Is Ethnicity? Everyone Has an Ethnicity, and You Don't Just Say American

Rawpixel.com/Shutterstock.com

Have you ever heard someone say they are "color blind?" What they may mean is that they don't think they notice race or ethnicity when interacting with other people. While this may sound like a nice sentiment, Sociologists would have a hard time believing that. The truth is, we live in a world where, for better or for worse, race and ethnicity are noticed.

It is important to understand the difference between race and ethnicity, and be able to identify that you have both.

Rawpixel.com/Shutterstock.com

Race is a classification made on appearance, mostly skin color. You can think of black or white as racial categories.

Ethnicity is different from race. It is made up of your heritage, where your ancestors are from. When it comes to ethnicity it is composed of both your father's side and your mother's side. For this reason, most people have a varied ethnic makeup.

You might say, "We should not care about race or ethnicity. We should just judge people for who they are on the inside." Remember that is not reflective of our true culture, though. There are many examples you can see of this. Think about when you fill out surveys or job applications. Have you had to fill one out recently? You would notice you are asked to check a box for your race and a box for your ethnicity. There is data being collected. Studies are done, and it helps to know where people are from, what types of people are applying for certain positions, and so on. Understand that not all discussion of race and ethnicity is done from a harmful place.

We will discuss racism later in this chapter, but for now, understand in order to function in our current culture there is an expectation one would know their race and ethnicity and be able to select them from a list of options.

2.   Culture and Ethnicity

Remember I mentioned most people would not have one ethnicity and only one. Your ethnicity is comprised of all the ethnic makeup of both parents. Within each person there is potential for great ethnic diversity. So how do most people choose an ethnicity to explain to other people?

It usually goes by culture. Think of what ethnicity you say you are. For example, when asked, I often say I am Italian. Does that mean I am one hundred percent Italian? No, it just means that is the part of my heritage I most closely identify with. Why is that? Growing up I heard my grandmother speak Italian. I was close with her, and she had a large impact on my life. She cooked traditional Italian meals and I learned about the culture from her. I was raised hearing stories from my mother of all of her Italian relatives and their family functions. This left an impression on me, and so this is the ethnicity I claim.

Ruslan Kalnitsky/Shutterstock.com

We give freedom for ethnicity to be self-declared. That is to say, just as I have done, each individual is given the freedom to choose how they want to identify their ethnicity. Understand that within that freedom there are sometimes certain limits. For example, if you are choosing your ethnicity for a job application, you will have to choose one of the listed options. If your chosen ethnic-

Valentyn Volkov/Shutterstock.com

ity is not listed as an option, you may find yourself having to select the category of "Other." This may not feel very good, but it is the only choice aside from abandoning your own ethnicity and choosing another "societally given" choice.

3.   Racism and Stereotypes, and Why They are Hard to Get Rid of

We now understand Sociologists accept society has races and ethnic groups as a means of classifying people and understanding their cultures. It would be a great thing if all people were treated equally regardless of their race or ethnicity, however unfortunately we know this is not the case. *Racism* occurs when someone makes judgments and assumptions about another person based on their race or ethnicity. Usually these judgments are asserting one's race is superior to another's. *Stereotypes* can occur when someone assumes certain characteristics or qualities about a person based on their race or ethnicity.

Stereotypes can be especially harmful due to the fact that many people are not even aware they are engaging in them. We have a society where our popular culture uses stereotypes frequently. You can think of many current examples of companies or celebrities who get into trouble for making statements containing stereotypes. Many comedians have even built their acts around sharing jokes that perpetuate stereotypical beliefs.

1tomm/Shutterstock.com

We have legal protections in place to protect individuals from racism and stereotypes. For example, in the workplace you are not supposed to make racist jokes or comments. People can lose their jobs if they are discriminating against others based on their race or ethnic background. Understand that even having these laws is evidence that this sort of conduct exists. We would not have these laws if people had not conducted this behavior in the first place. Minorities in the United States have expressed a great deal of problems in many areas of society, stemming from racist beliefs and actions. Some people are not even open to having minority groups express these experiences. This poses a great challenge to opening the dialogue, and hopefully changing the world to be less biased. We will discuss this more at the end of the chapter, when we tune in societal change and progress.

4. Religion

Religion is another area of life where we allow people the freedom to choose how they want to identify and express themselves. We have organized religions, which are groups who join together in worship and agree on similar beliefs on God, the afterlife, and so on. The most common organized religion in the United States in Christianity. Christianity is based on the teachings of Jesus Christ and follows the text called The Bible. In the United States, the government

SantiPhotoSS/Shutterstock.com

opted to make the right to choose your religion and express it a protected right. This is not the case everywhere in the world. It is important to note that religion is a very deeply personal issue for many people. Some feel as though their path is the one and only true way, and they are willing to fight for their way to the death. There have been many battles fought over religion, and religious tensions remain in many areas of the world today.

In the United States, the government has also chosen to have what they call a "separation of church and state." What this means is that the government is supposed to operate without a religious affiliation. However, many would disagree that this is truly the way things work. For example, take a look at a dollar bill, no let's make that a one-hundred-dollar bill to be more fun. What do you see written on it?

9george/Shutterstock.com

"In God we trust."

Why would our money, one of the most important and valuable things in our culture, say something about God on it, if we truly have a separation of church and state? Do the people who don't believe in God have less of a right to possess money in our society?

You have to understand, religion infuses itself into our government and our culture in many ways. Despite what some may try to claim, it is easy to see examples. Think of the holidays most employers honor. Ever heard of a certain common holiday called Christmas?

Is everyone in every workplace Christian? Does everyone choose to celebrate Christmas and therefore needs this day off as a day of worship? Of course this is not the case, however, due to the dominant religion in our culture being Christianity, those holidays are most regularly observed.

What happens if you are in our society and choose to not have a religion? What if you do not believe in the presence of a God at all? You will likely be judged by some people if you outwardly express your lack

Guschenkova/Shutterstock.com

of faith. There is an assumption by some religious people that those who do not have a religion lack a moral compass. Some seek their moral and ideological framework through the confines of an organized religion. If that is the case, they may be skeptical someone could truly be a "good person" without religion. On the other hand, some people who do not believe in God see those who follow religions as "brainwashed" or weak minded. It is important to remember that in our society there are many diverse religious and spiritual beliefs.

Spirituality allows for someone to believe in a higher power, in the universe or the presence of something greater, without the need for a specific path. There is no need for an individual who calls themselves spiritual to state their religion, as they may not have an organized religion they align with. We are seeing trends of more open and flexible spiritual beliefs, with freedom to pick and choose the truths that align with a person's own belief system. Some say the spiritual path is a much more open minded and positive way to live. What do you think about spirituality versus religion?

5.   Societal Progress

We have seen a great deal of societal change and progress in the area of racism and religious judgment, and it is the hope of Sociologists that we would continue to move forward with this progress.

It isn't a given that society will change on its own. What is required for great change is a great amount of effort by the people. We are given a right to peaceful protest in our American society. We have seen recent movements to utilize this power to speak out against injustice. It isn't always easy to be heard. Not everyone is open to changing society. It is very uncomfortable to have some of these discussions, and therefore there are many times when opportu-

Dave Hewison Photography/Shutterstock.com

nities for change go without being utilized. Sociology can help empower people to make change, by pointing out the injustices, and giving people the tools to present them in a clear and concise way. For example, it is helpful when attempting to show racism exists to have evidence. Someone could present data on the remarks certain individuals in a certain profession have made, and show that there are many biased beliefs in that profession. Change can happen, and Sociology is a vital tool for social action and greater social justice.

Activity 17: Your Race and Your Ethnicity

Now that you know the difference between race and ethnicity, think about how you would define yours.

Rawpixel.com/Shutterstock.com

What is your race?

What is your ethnicity?

How does your ethnicity impact your life?

In what cultural ways do you interact with your ethnicity? List a few examples.

Activity 18: Religion

Do you have a religion?

Halfpoint/Shutterstock.com

If you do, what is your religion?

If you do not have a religion, how has this impacted your life? Has this impacted the way people treat you?

What are your thoughts on spirituality versus organized religion?

CHAPTER 10

Capitalism and the Economy

1. Analyze US Government
2. Types of Government
3. Caste System
4. Social Mobility

1. Analyze US Government

We are winding down our time together, and one of the last areas of society you need to make sure you understand from a Sociological perspective is a very important one: the government. When you take the time to really think about it, you realize how much power and control your government has over you and your daily life. It's much more than who is elected president, though of course that has an impact as well. It has to do with the laws and rules and values and ideology of the culture—all of that is affected in a big way by the government. To help us better understand the depth of impact the government has on the lives of its citizens, we will use the United States as an example and walk through some areas.

You can tell a lot about a government and its values by what it chooses to spend its money on. In

Andrea Izzotti/Shutterstock.com

our culture we are willing to spend tax money to provide kindergarten through twelfth grade. In fact, think about it this way—every tax payer has to spend their money toward educating children, even if they don't have any of their own.

Imagine if I tried to say, "Hey government, since I don't have any kids, can I have that money back? I want to spend it on something I choose." That is

Monkey Business Images/Shutterstock.com

not an outrageous question, right? It makes sense people would want their hard-earned money to go toward things that directly benefit them. However, you have to realize we have a government and a society where there is a high value placed on education. We want a society full of people who have a certain education level, and therefore we are willing to put our money toward that goal. Compare that to something we are unwilling to spend our tax money on—health care.

We have a system of government where we want people to work hard, and to be able to support themselves. Having this system of Capitalism, which we will examine more in the next section, we have a culture based around the ideology that people can't be given everything by the government. Though we do provide education, we do not provide health care. If you want to have access to a hospital or doctor, you should purchase your own insurance. This is what our society has decided on.

Note that not everywhere else in the world has made the same decisions when it comes to providing their citizens with health care, and there are many people within the United States who wish things would change. However, when you learn more about the system of Capitalism you can see why it would not necessarily lend itself to providing such support to its citizens.

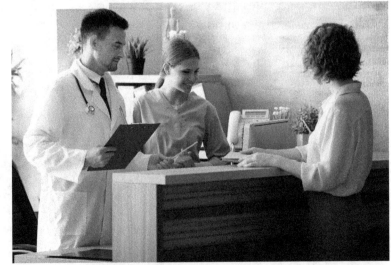

Africa Studio/Shutterstock.com

2.   Types of Government

Capitalism is the system of government we have in the United States.
The key thing to remember here is
that it is both a political and an eco-
nomic system. What that means is
that our laws, rules, culture, and
ideology are all formed around the
framework of Capitalism. What are
some of the key components of this
system? Well, first and foremost you
have to understand what the society
runs on—money.

bluedog studio/Shutterstock.com

Remember here that there is no one perfect form of government, so this is not to be overly
critical of Capitalism. However, it would be unfair to analyze the system without admitting there
is a heavy emphasis on money. Some critics say Capitalism places money before all else, including God, family, or any morality. Money is necessary to survive in a capitalist society, and there
are inherent "winners" and "losers" when you let competition exist in the marketplace.

Socialism would differ from Capitalism in that the government would provide more services
to the citizens. The biggest drawback of Socialism as it compares to Capitalism, and the fear
of many of us in our society moving more toward Socialist systems is the higher taxation. You
have to remember what our country was built upon—people leaving England who were upset
with unfair taxation. As a nation we are opposed to raising taxes unless there is a very compel-
ling reason. We do offer some services to assist people who are dealing with financial hardship,
without being a Socialist nation. This would include welfare programs, housing assistance, and
so on. In a Socialist system, as opposed to Capitalist, the government has control over the econ-
omy. Socialism is placed in between Capitalism and a more greatly differing government system,
Communism.

Communism is a system where there
would not be a need for private property
or ownership. The public would share
the means of production. This system
would vary greatly from the United
States and our system of Capitalism.
Although Capitalism has a big focus
on obtaining money and competition, Communism would have none of
that same focus. If you are invested
in the ideology of Capitalism, then
Communism would seek shocking and
perhaps even "wrong." Those who are

g-stockstuido/Shutterstock.com

in support of Communism would be critical of Capitalism and point out the greed and inequality in the system as evidence that it is an unjust way of living.

A **dictatorship** is an authoritarian system of government run by one individual. This would contrast greatly from the United States system of government, where there are purposeful checks and balances in place. A dictator has an immense amount of power, and there are many examples throughout history of these individuals using their

XiXinXing/Shutterstock.com

power in harmful ways. In the United States, the government has taken precautions to ensure against rule by a dictator, including allowing citizens to vote freely in elections and limiting terms of government officials, including the president.

3. Caste System

A caste system is a system of society where there are assigned roles. Individuals cannot change their social class, no matter what actions they take. This would differ from a captialist society, where the focus would be on obtaining money and bettering one's position in society. Think of the ideology of the "American dream." We are taught that hard work and dedication will always equal out to a better life. Even though there is evidence that this may not really be the case, that life is not fair from the start, and that there are many blocks in the way for many people, the ideology of the dream persists.

MaxyM/Shutterstock.com

Contrast the belief of the "American dream" with the caste system society, where there would be no need for a dream of a better life. People are dealt their life position at birth, and there is no amount of hard work on their end that can change it. Many people within a Capitalist society would have great criticisms of this system, but can you see how those within the caste system would view Capitalism? Differing systems would be taught their way is the right way, and find it hard to understand

Prostock-studio/Shutterstock.com

how others could live the way they do. Instead of wanting to be a part of a caste system, members of a Capitalist society would pride themselves on their ability to have social mobility.

4. Social Mobility

Social mobility allows members of a society to change their social class and status. The easiest way to think about social mobility is to say if you make more money your life will change. More money equals more access to buying more expensive things, living in a different neighborhood, access to other wealthy people, and so on. Social mobility does not have to go upward, however. You can lose a job, lose your home, lose a great deal of money in the stock market—and then what would you have? You would have a lower social status, and downward social mobility.

For obvious reasons, most people in society would hope for upward mobility. As we do not have a fixed class system such as a caste system, we allow for individuals to improve their life circumstances. However, critics would state that life still is not totally fair, and that hard work does not necessarily guarantee one improving their social class. There are many biases in place in society. The wealthy begin their lives at an advantage, and we see wealth passed down among generations. Starting out in a low social status, it is much more difficult to rise up. Statistically speaking, most people do not have rapid social movement, but rather move up or down a single class. Are you hoping to have social mobility in your life? What are you doing to ensure you will continue to move up in society, working hard to better yourself? I truly wish you all the best as you overcome the obstacles on your pathway to greater success.

Activity 19: US Government

Do you have positive thoughts about the US government?

What about your negative thoughts? What changes would you like to see happen to the US government?

Sean Locke Photography/Shutterstock.com

What do you think about the system of Capitalism?

What would you think about the United States switching to a system of Socialism?

What about switching to a system of Communism?

What are your thoughts on dictators?

Activity 20: Social Mobility

Give an example from your own life of a time you have experienced upward mobility.

Gennady Danilkin/Shutterstock.com

How did it feel to increase your wealth or status?

How would it feel to have downward mobility?

Would you be willing to assist others if you had rapid upward social mobility? What if you made millions of dollars?

Should the government force those who make extreme amounts of wealth to share it with others who have less?

Why or why not?

CHAPTER 11
Social Movements and Change

1. Social Movements
2. How Social Movements Create Change
3. Hippies
4. Civil Rights and Civil Disobedience
5. Women's Rights
6. MeToo and Social Media Movements
7. What Still Needs to Change?

1. Social Movements

Now that you have a greater understanding of the way Sociology works, we can put it together into the examples that truly best tie it together—**social movements**. Social movements combine a cause with action in order to create social change. There are many examples of social movements throughout history, and we will explore a few key ones. You can measure the effectiveness of a social movement. Did the movement create change in the world? Was the change long lasting? Did the movement bring awareness to an issue or inequality? This is how Sociology has the power to truly change the world.

2. How Social Movements Create Change

When people get together in groups, there is great power. The possibility for change with the assistance of numbers is great. This is how social movements are able to create change. If you are involved in a peaceful protest, and there are enough people who join the protest, you will be noticed. Think about how difficult it would be to get people to listen, to truly notice, without the help of a large group. Social movements rely on the group tactic to spread. Once a movement takes off, others around notice it, and are likely to join up.

A movement must have a clear goal— there is something going on in society and people are not happy about it. After considering it, people decide they want to take a stand, they want to help make a difference. People in social movements are willing to take time out of their lives in order to focus on a better world for everyone around them. Some even risk getting arrested for the causes they believe in. Without people being willing to do something, to come together and work on the world, changes would not happen. It is up to the people to take back their power and create lasting change on the quest to make the world a better place.

Lucky Business/Shutterstock.com

johnny chaos/Shutterstock.com

3. Hippies

The hippies and the summer of love are by far my favorite social movements. I love this time period, and feel it truly is the best way to illustrate some of the Sociological concepts in the real world. During this time period, people were upset about many different areas of society. You had the United States fighting a war, the Vietnam War, where men were not given a choice, they were drafted to go and fight, potentially to their death. Can you image what that would feel like? Shouldn't people be given a choice as to if they agree with the ideology of a war, agree with the idea of "kill or be killed" before they are forced into it?

Aside from the war, there were conflicts within the culture of the society. Hippies were a countercultural movement. They were a reaction to the conservative, old school views. People, a lot of them young college students, wanted to be able to expand their minds and live in a more peaceful world. They were disregarded and dismissed in many cases due to the way they dressed, the way they wore their hair, the way they spoke—all of which was not in alignment with the traditional norms of society.

An Vino/Shutterstock.com

However, it was not all merely superficial. Behind the colorful tie-dye and the long-haired men were some substantial and impactful beliefs on society. Woodstock was a large concert which occurred during this time period, where people assembled to listen to music and reflect on peace and love. The social movement of the hippies was a beautiful attempt at making the world a better place. I would love to see a world where this movement had continued on in a greater volume, I truly think it would be a groovy and peaceful world for all.

Forty3Zero/Shutterstock.com

4. Civil Rights and Civil Disobedience

The civil rights movements were a wonderful example of people refusing to obey the unjust laws of society. Here is an important Sociological truth: Just because something is a law, does not mean it is right. People should not be treated differently based on the color of their skin. Yes, you might say, of course that is true. However, understand it was not too long ago when that belief was not the dominant one in society. In order to create social change and make the world more equal for all people, regardless of skin color, there were major social movements.

Civil disobedience was utilized during the civil rights movement. This requires people to purposefully break the laws, and suffer any and all consequences, in order to illustrate the need to change the structure of society. When Rosa Parks refused to sit in the back of the bus, she was not only taking a stand for the rights of others, she was taking on the personal consequences.

It takes great bravery to be willing to risk yourself for the betterment of society. Civil disobedience is an incredibly effective tool for social change.

5. Women's Rights

Many people forget how hard women have had to fight for an equal place in society. In face, in many places in the world women would still not be considered equal to men. There are many ways you can measure equality. One would be voting, and women earned that right much later than men in the United States. Another right would be the right to equal pay, and women are actually still working on this in the United States, as the wage gap between men and women for the same positions still exists.

How did women get a better place within society? They had to fight for it. By "fight" for it I don't mean go to literal war. I mean they had to band together, in great numbers, and refuse to allow society to continue along the way it had been.

Everett Historical/Shutterstock.com

Mihai Surdu/Shutterstock.com

If they were to stay silent, things would not have changed on their own. You have learned about power previously; you know that those in power are the comfortable ones in society. The people in power do not want to give their power away freely. It takes great convincing on the part of the less powerful in order to get more equal treatment. This is where the effectiveness of a social movement is so important.

6. MeToo and Social Media Movements

We have seen some current social movements that rely heavily on the use of social media. One example is the MeToo movement. This movement used a hashtag to spread personal stories of women's victimization. Women wanted to speak out about sexual violence, about the harassment and mistreatment they have faced in society. Through sharing their stories, the movement gained momentum.

People would not have ordinarily shared such deeply personal experiences if not for feeling comfortable. We are seeing social media creating meaningful dialogue. It is beyond the superficial expectations many had for what social media could offer. In fact, social media allows for connection and conversation. We will see many more movements which rely on social media to help spread their messages and bond people together in the quest to change outdated beliefs and systems.

7. What Still Needs to Change?

Now you are equipped with all the tools to create your own social movements. You will be asked to do so in one of the exercises below. Remember that the starting place is some sort of problem in the world, something where you find yourself looking around and questioning, "Does it have to be this way?" Please always remember that, no, it does not have to be that way. Society is comprised of people, people hold the true power to change it. Change is always possible. Change is necessary, in fact. Society should always be moving in the direction of more justice, more fairness, more equality, and more kindness.

The true fix for all problems? Love. If you can remove your biases, your judgments, all of the things we shed light on previously in our time together, you will find that what exists underneath them is the same for every human—love. It is possible for the world as we know it to look very different. An awakening is possible, but it will require people to get comfortable discussing uncomfortable truths. That's where Sociology comes in. You can use a scientific process to give credibility to your claims for more justice. You can show data that backs up your points, you can combine logic and reason with emotion. And with love, always, always combine with love.

Activity 21: Pick a Past Social Movement and Analyze

Pick your social movement and list it here.

Toronto-Images Com/Shutterstock.com

What was the social movement based on? What was the issue?

What tactics did the movement use?

Who was involved in the movement?

Was the movement successful?

Why or why not?

Activity 22: Design Your Own Social Movement

Identify an area of social life you'd like to change.

In your ideal society, how does it now function?

Polarpx/Shutterstock.com

How do we get there?

What tactics does your social movement use?

How do you spread your message?

What is your slogan?

Who is a part of your movement?

CPSIA information can be obtained
at www.ICGtesting.com
Printed in the USA
LVHW050425150820
663264LV00001B/3

9 781524 960766